BE A SCIENTIST
LET'S INVESTIGATE
MATERIALS

JACQUI BAILEY

CRABTREE
PUBLISHING COMPANY
WWW.CRABTREEBOOKS.COM

CRABTREE
PUBLISHING COMPANY
WWW.CRABTREEBOOKS.COM

Author: Jacqui Bailey

Editorial director: Kathy Middleton

Series editor: Julia Bird

Editor: Ellen Rodger

Illustrator: Ed Myer

Packaged by: Collaborate

Proofreader: Petrice Custance

**Production coordinator
and Prepress technician:** Ken Wright

Print coordinator: Katherine Berti

Library and Achives Canada Cataloguing in Publication

Title: Let's investigate materials / Jacqui Bailey.
Other titles: Investigating materials
Names: Bailey, Jacqui, author.
Description: Series statement: Be a scientist |
  Previously published under title: Investigating materials. |
  Includes index.
Identifiers: Canadiana (print) 20200354590 |
  Canadiana (ebook) 20200354612 |
  ISBN 9781427127754 (hardcover) |
  ISBN 9781427127815 (softcover) |
  ISBN 9781427127877 (HTML)
Subjects: LCSH: Matter—Properties—Juvenile literature. |
  LCSH: Matter—Properties—Experiments—Juvenile literature.
Classification: LCC QC173.36 .B35 2021 | DDC j530—dc23

Library of Congress Cataloging-in-Publication Data

Names: Bailey, Jacqui, author.
Title: Let's investigate materials / Jacqui Bailey.
Description: New York, NY : Crabtree Publishing Company, 2021. |
  Series: Be a scientist | Includes index.
Identifiers: LCCN 2020045167 (print) | LCCN 2020045168 (ebook) |
  ISBN 9781427127754 (hardcover) |
  ISBN 9781427127815 (paperback) |
  ISBN 9781427127877 (ebook)
Subjects: LCSH: Materials--Juvenile literature.
Classification: LCC TA403.2 .B344 2021 (print) |
  LCC TA403.2 (ebook) | DDC 620.1/1--dc23
LC record available at https://lccn.loc.gov/2020045167
LC ebook record available at https://lccn.loc.gov/2020045168

Crabtree Publishing Company

www.crabtreebooks.com   1–800–387–7650

Published in 2021 by Crabtree Publishing Company

First published in Great Britain in 2019 by Wayland
Copyright © Hodder & Stoughton, 2019

Printed in the U.S.A./122020/CG20201014

Every attempt has been made to clear copyright. Should there be any inadvertent omission please apply to the publisher for rectification.

**Published in Canada
Crabtree Publishing**
616 Welland Ave.
St. Catharines, Ontario
L2M 5V6

**Published in the United States
Crabtree Publishing**
347 Fifth Avenue
Suite 1402–145
New York, NY 10016

BE A SCIENTIST

LET'S INVESTIGATE
MATERIALS

CRABTREE
PUBLISHING COMPANY
WWW.CRABTREEBOOKS.COM

CONTENTS

WHAT ARE MATERIALS?

Materials are the substances that things are made of. Your clothes are made from a group of materials called **fabrics**. But everything else in the world is made from materials, too.

THINK about all the different materials there are.
• The chair you are sitting on might be made of wood or plastic.
• This book is made from paper. What other types of material can you see around you?

YOU WILL NEED
A sheet of paper
A pencil and a ruler
A group of objects made from different materials (e.g. your school bag and all the objects inside it)

WHAT ARE THINGS MADE OF?

1 Use the pencil and ruler to draw a line down the middle of the paper.

2 In the left-hand column, make a list of all the different objects you have.

3 In the right-hand column, write down the materials you think each object is made from.

pencil	wood, graphite
pen	plastic, ink
book	paper
ruler	

" BECAUSE...

We use so many different materials because each one is made differently and behaves in different ways. Nylon is a type of plastic that is strong and bends well. It is used to make ropes. Metal is strong and stiff, so we use it to make spoons. "

4 Remember that some objects, such as a pencil, may be made from more than one material. Ask an adult if you are not sure what a material is called.

5 How many materials did you find? In each case, why do you think that material was used and not another?

HARD OR SOFT?

Some materials are hard and strong. Some are soft and squishy. We use them in different ways.

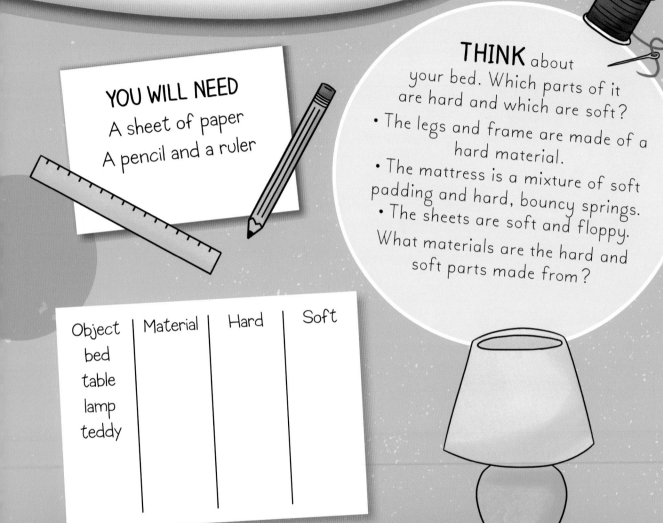

YOU WILL NEED

A sheet of paper

A pencil and a ruler

THINK about your bed. Which parts of it are hard and which are soft?

- The legs and frame are made of a hard material.
- The mattress is a mixture of soft padding and hard, bouncy springs.
- The sheets are soft and floppy.

What materials are the hard and soft parts made from?

Object	Material	Hard	Soft
bed			
table			
lamp			
teddy			

WHICH MATERIALS ARE HARD AND WHICH ARE SOFT?

1 Use the ruler to divide your paper into four columns and label them with the headings above.

2 Look at the objects in a room such as your bedroom. List all the objects in the first column, and the materials they are made from in the second.

3 Is each material hard or soft? Put a checkmark for each object in the "hard" column or the "soft" column. Why do you think that hard materials were used instead of soft materials for some objects?

"BECAUSE...

Hard materials, such as metal and wood, are useful because they are strong and keep their shape. They are good for building with or supporting weight, so we use them to make furniture. Soft materials bend and wrap around different shapes, so we use them to make comfortable clothes and bedding. "

STRETCH AND SQUEEZE

Some materials are **elastic**. This means that they can be pulled or squashed into different shapes. Then, when you let them go, they snap back into their original shape.

YOU WILL NEED
A sheet of paper
A pencil and a ruler
A selection of different clothing (e.g. a pair of tights, a wool hat, a T-shirt, a raincoat, a swimsuit)

THINK about some things that are elastic.
- A sponge squashes.
- An elastic band stretches.
- Lots of clothes are stretchy.

Find out more about stretchy fabrics.

WHICH FABRICS ARE THE STRETCHIEST?

1 Divide your paper into three columns. Name your columns: clothing, stretch, and material.

2 Write the names of your test clothing in the first column.

" BECAUSE...

Some fabrics stretch more than others because they are made from a mixture of materials. Some of the stretchiest fabrics include a material called spandex. This material lets fabrics stretch and return to shape.
The more a fabric stretches, the more spandex it has in it.

"

Clothing	Stretch	Material
t-shirt	2	cotton
hat	2	wool
tights	3	spandex
raincoat	1	

3 Tug on each piece of clothing to test it for stretchiness. Mark it 1 for no stretch, 2 for some stretch, and 3 for lots of stretch.

4 Now check the labels inside each piece of clothing to see what materials it is made from. Write down the materials in the third column. Which fabrics are the stretchiest?

DOES IT BEND?

Some materials bend, but others do not. Bendable materials are called **flexible**. Materials that do not bend easily are described as **rigid**.

YOU WILL NEED

A selection of different materials (e.g. a straw for drinking, a wooden pencil, a piece of string, a birthday cake candle, paper, a metal coat hanger, a metal spoon, a plastic fork, a spatula)
A pencil and a sheet of paper

THINK about things that are bendable and things that are not.
- Cotton thread is very flexible and good for sewing things together.
- A sewing needle made from metal is rigid, so it can push through fabric.
Which materials are flexible and which are not?

WHICH MATERIALS ARE BENDY?

1 Starting with the straw, try to bend each object.

2 Note the materials that bend easily, those that are hard to bend, and those that break!

3 Make a list of the reasons why you think we need bendable materials and why we need stiff materials.

4 Compare your list with a friend's.

" BECAUSE...

Flexible materials are useful because we can bend or fold them into any shape we want. Rigid materials are useful because they keep their shape when you use them. Some rigid materials are very strong, but others break easily when we bend them. We say these materials are **brittle**. "

THINK
about using:
- Wood to make shoelaces.
- Paper to make a stepladder.

What do you think would happen?

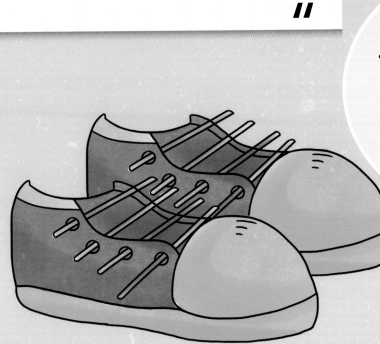

SHINY OR DULL?

Some materials are shiny and some are dull.

THINK about how some materials **reflect**, or bounce back, more light than others. Which materials reflect the most light?

YOU WILL NEED

A pencil and paper

SHINY

DULL

WHAT MAKES MATERIALS SHINY?

"

BECAUSE...

Smooth, polished materials shine the most because more light bounces straight off them. Rough materials scatter light, so they look dull.

"

1 Look around a room. How many things can you find that reflect light? What materials are they made from?

2 Now look for objects that do not reflect light. What materials are they made from?

3 Make lists of your shiny and dull materials and compare them. Which materials are smooth and which are rough?

WHAT MAKES MATERIALS DULL?

THINK
about what happens when a smooth surface becomes dusty. Is it still shiny?

1. Carefully cut a piece of foil and look at its shinier side. Can you see your reflection in it?

2. Now crumple up the foil and roughly straighten it out again. What happens?

3. Smear some butter on another piece of foil. Is it still as shiny as it was?

YOU WILL NEED
Aluminum foil
Some butter

" BECAUSE...
The foil was shiniest when it was smooth and clean because it reflected the light well. We use materials that reflect light well to make mirrors. Mirrors are made by placing a smooth piece of glass on top of a thin layer of shiny metal. **"**

SEE THROUGH?

Some materials are **transparent**, meaning we can see right through them. Some are **opaque**. This means we cannot see through them at all. Other materials are **translucent**. Things look blurry through them.

YOU WILL NEED

A cardboard tube (e.g. the inner tube from a roll of toilet paper)
Tape or elastic bands
Test materials (e.g. paper, cotton cloth, a tissue, plastic wrap, a plastic bag, metal foil, tracing paper, felt, a candy wrapper)
A pencil and paper

THINK about things that are transparent, opaque, and translucent.

• Clear glass is transparent.
• Most clothing is opaque!
• Wax paper is translucent.

Look at some materials and decide how much you can see through them.

WHICH MATERIALS CAN YOU SEE THROUGH?

1 Hold the cardboard tube up to one eye, like a telescope. Check if you can see clearly through it.

2 Wrap each test material over one end of the tube. Do this one at a time. Hold the test material in place with tape or elastic bands. Look through the tube. Can see through the material?

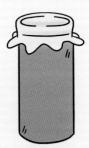

3 Which test materials can you see through? Is what you see clear or fuzzy?

4 Make a list of which test materials are transparent, which are translucent, and which are opaque.

BECAUSE...

"Transparent materials, such as glass and clear plastic, are useful. Light can pass through them but other things cannot. Glass windows let light into a building but they keep out the rain. Clear plastic storage containers allow us to see what is inside them without having to open them."

WATERPROOF?

Some materials are **waterproof**. This means liquids roll off them. But other materials are **absorbent** and liquids soak into them.

THINK about what happens when it is raining.
- Rain runs off of pavement.
- Rain soaks into the soil.

What waterproof materials can you think of?

IS IT WATERPROOF?

1. Fill the cup halfway with water.

2. Wrap each piece of material over the top of the cup, one after the other. Hold it tightly in place with the elastic bands.

3. Turn the cup upside down over the bowl. What happens with each material?

18

CAN YOU MAKE IT WATERPROOF?

1 Rub a candle over a dry piece of cotton cloth so that it becomes well waxed (you might need an adult to help you soften the candle a little).

2 Now put the cloth over the cup of water, as before, waxed side out. Does the candle wax make a difference?

" BECAUSE...

Waterproof materials are useful because they allow us to keep things dry, and to store and carry liquids. Absorbent materials are useful for cleaning things or rubbing them dry. "

THINK about
the clothing you wear in the rain. Unlike most of your clothing, they are waterproof. Often an extra material is added to the fabric.

19

FLOAT OR SINK?

Some things float easily in water, and some do not. Find out which materials float and which materials sink.

YOU WILL NEED

A pencil and paper

A large plastic bowl or tank filled with water

A group of objects made from different materials (e.g. a nail, a marble, an apple, a bath sponge, a wooden spoon, a coin, a cork, a sheet of paper towel)

A lump of modeling clay.

WILL IT FLOAT OR SINK?

1 Make a list of your objects and write down which ones you think will sink and which will float.

2 Put them in the water one at a time and see if you were right.

3 Make a note of the objects that float, and the objects that sink straight to the bottom. Are the objects that sink similar in any way?

"BECAUSE...

Small, heavy objects, such as metal coins and glass marbles, sink straight to the bottom. Materials such as wood and cork float because they are light for their size and waterproof. An absorbent material, such as a paper towel, may float at first. As it soaks up water, it then sinks. "

CAN YOU MAKE IT FLOAT?

1 Try floating a lump of modeling clay. Then pat it dry.

2 Roll it out so that it is wide and flat. Fold up the sides a little to make a boat shape.

3 Now carefully place it on the water. Does it float or sink?

THINK about a large ship.

• It is made from metal, just like a coin.

• It is a very different shape from a coin.

Do you think the ship's shape helps it to float?

HOT OR COLD?

Heat travels easily through some materials. These materials warm up more quickly than others.

YOU WILL NEED

A wooden spoon, a metal spoon, and a plastic spoon, all the same length
Some butter
3 peas
A heatproof jug
A saucepan of hot water
An adult to help

THINK about how heat travels from a hot material to a colder one when someone makes you a hot drink.

- The hot liquid heats up the cold cup.
- The heat travels into the air around the cup and the liquid and they become cooler. Soon you can pick up the cup, and drink the liquid.

Can you see heat travel from one material to another?

HOW CAN YOU SEE HEAT TRAVEL?

1   Use a small lump of butter to glue one pea to the end of each spoon handle.

2 Carefully stand the three spoons upright in the jug, with the peas at the top.

3 Ask an adult to pour a little hot water into the base of the jug. Make it no deeper than the round parts of the spoons.

4 Which pea is the first one to fall? Which is the last?

THINK about a metal pan with a wooden handle.
- Metal heats up quickly so that food will cook.
- The wood stays cool so the cook can pick up the pan.

A material that heat travels through slowly is called an **insulator**.

" BECAUSE...

The peas fell off because heat from the water traveled up the spoons and melted the butter. The pea fell off the metal spoon first because heat travels quickly through metal. We say that metal is a good **conductor** of heat. "

23

MADE BY NATURE

Many of the materials we use are **natural materials**-they come from living things, or from Earth itself.

YOU WILL NEED
A piece of cardboard
Scissors
Two different colors of wool
A darning needle

THINK about different natural materials.

• Wood used for furniture and buildings comes from trees.
• Clay and sand come from rocks and soil.
• Wool used for knitting and weaving cloth comes from sheep.

How can you make a piece of wool into a piece of cloth?

HOW DOES WOOL MAKE CLOTH?

1 Cut small triangular teeth into the two longest edges of the cardboard. You may need an adult to help you with this.

2 Loop one color wool around one end of the cardboard and tie a knot. Wind the wool along the cardboard so that each loop sits in one of the teeth (see page 25). This is called the warp thread.

3 Thread the needle with the other color wool. Use the needle to pull the wool under and over each of the warp threads. At the end of one row, turn the needle around and work back in the opposite direction. This is the weft thread.

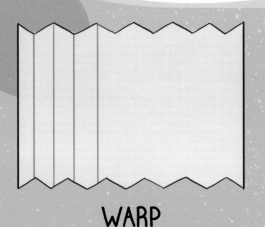

WARP

WEFT

4 As you do each row, push it up gently so that it sits closely to the row next to it.

5 When you have filled one side of the cardboard, knot the end of your weft thread. Then cut along the middle of the warp threads on the back of the cardboard and take your woven cloth off it.

" BECAUSE...

Natural materials are useful because we can make all kinds of things from them. Sometimes we change a material's shape, such as turning fleece into woollen yarn. We can also break up a material, such as by chopping wood. But the material itself does not change. "

MAKING MATERIALS

Some natural materials can be changed into other types of materials. These materials would not exist if people did not make them. They are known as **human-made materials**.

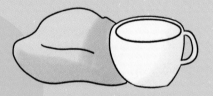

THINK about how we change natural materials into human-made materials.

- Sand is heated up and turned to glass.
- Clay is shaped, baked, and glazed to make china.
- Oil is used to make all kinds of plastics, such as polythene, polyester, and nylon.
- Wood is chopped and then boiled to make paper.

There are many ways to change one material into another.

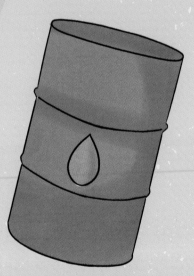

YOU WILL NEED

A block of modeling clay
A rolling pin
A strip of cardstock about 2 inches (5 cm) wide and 20 inches (50 cm) long
Plaster of Paris powder
A clean jug
Water

CAN YOU MAKE A SOFT MATERIAL INTO A HARD ONE?

1 Roll out the clay into a round, flat base, about 0.4 inches (1 cm) thick, or a little bigger than your hand.

2 Press your flat hand firmly into the clay. Lift up your hand so that you leave its shape printed in the clay.

3 Curve the strip of cardstock into a circle that fits around your handprint. Press it gently into the clay.

4 Put some plaster of Paris in the jug and mix it with water until you have a creamy paste.

5 Pour the paste into the card circle so that it completely covers the handprint. Leave the paste to dry.

6 When the paste is completely dry, peel away the clay and the cardstock. You are left with a hard plaster model of your hand.

" BECAUSE...

The plaster of Paris changed from a soft powder into a hard plaster because it was mixed with water and left in the open air. Many materials are changed by mixing them with other materials. Sometimes they change when they are heated. "

GLOSSARY

Absorbent
materials, such as sponges and paper towels, soak up liquids.

Brittle
materials are hard, but they shatter or break easily if they are bent or smashed. Glass and china are both brittle materials.

Conductors
are materials that allow heat to pass through them easily. They heat up and cool down quickly. Metals are good conductors.

Some materials do not just absorb water, they also soak up other things. A thick, dark cloth will absorb heat, light, and sound.

Elastic
materials are stretchy and springy. These materials can be pulled or squashed out of their original shape, but return to it when they are let go. Rubber and spandex are elastic materials.

Fabrics
are the cloths we make from different materials. Cotton, wool, and nylon cloth are all fabrics.

Flexible
materials are easily bent and folded. Unlike elastic materials, they do not naturally return to their original shape. Paper, copper wire, and some plastics are flexible.

Human-made materials
are materials that have been produced by people. Paper and plastics are human-made.

Insulators
are materials that do not allow heat to pass through them easily. Insulators can be used to keep heat in or out. Wood and some plastics are good insulators.

Natural materials

grow from living things or are part of Earth itself. Wood, oil, and rock are all natural materials.

Opaque

materials do not allow any light to pass through them. Most materials are opaque, so we cannot see through them.

Reflection

happens when light bounces off the surface of a material. If the surface is very smooth, it reflects light and we can sometimes see an image of ourselves or other objects in it.

Rigid

materials cannot bend or fold. Wood is a rigid material.

Translucent

materials allow some light to pass through them, but they also reflect some light. You can see through them but only in a blurry way. Tracing paper is translucent.

Transparent

materials allow light to pass through them. Colorless glass and water are transparent. You can see through them.

Waterproof

materials do not soak up liquids. Instead, liquids stay on the surface of the material and cannot pass through it. Materials such as metal, glass, and some plastics are waterproof.

Another word for materials that are human-made is artificial. We also say some human-made materials are synthetic. These materials are made in factories. Some fabrics are synthetics.

LEARNING MORE

BOOKS

Martin, Claudia. *Materials*. Capstone Press, 2018.

Sjonger, Rebecca. *Exploring Materials in My Makerspace*. Crabtree Publishing, 2018.

Sjonger, Rebecca. *Mixing and Separating Materials in My Makerspace*. Crabtree Publishing, 2018.

WEBSITES

www.science-sparks.com/category/key-stage-2-science/materials-and-their-properties-key-stage-2/ has experiments, worksheets, and STEM challenges.

Visit this site to learn more about materials: www.bbc.com/bitesize/topics/zryycdm.

PLACES TO VISIT

The Museum of Science in Boston has exhibits that deal with a huge variety of materials. You can also join online STEM learning sessions. Check the museum out at: www.mos.org.

Visit Chicago's Museum of Science and Industry to explore displays on materials and objects or take part in science labs and create things from different materials.

NOTE TO PARENTS AND TEACHERS:

Every effort has been made by the publisher to ensure that these websites contain no inappropriate or offensive material. However, because of the nature of the Internet, it is impossible to guarantee that the content of these sites will not be altered. We strongly advise that Internet access is supervised by a responsible adult.

INDEX